Early Application
for my Next Life

poems by John Clark Vincent

Cover and interior design by Lisa D. Holmes
(Yulan Studio, yulanstudio.com)

Published in Portland, Oregon by Yulan Studio, Inc.
Printed in the United States

First edition
ISBN: 979-8-9863990-2-7

… because everything is one thing

Acknowledgements

Thank you to:

Lisa D. Holmes for her love, support, graphic design and publishing business, creative recipes, adventurous spirit, soft skin, silky hair, and dreamy eyes.

Fellow writers Aileen Sheedy, Matteo Merenda, Waka T. Brown, Linda Bybee Kapfer, Cheryl Duffy, and Riley Glissendorf for their support, encouragement, and willingness to read my stuff and find things to like about it.

My mother and father who gave me lots of source material.

The neighborhood skunks who dug the yellowjacket nest out of my garden. They deserve a mention just as much as the squirrels, who are super cute, but whose excavation work is typically less productive.

Table of Contents

Section I - Poseur Sonnets

Early Application For My Next Life

Understanding that the competition
will be fierce, I decided to apply
early for my next life. This one's near done.
So using what's left to help clarify

my desires for the decision makers,
whoever they are, can't hurt my chances.
And, of course, I'll need to delineate
all my credentials. Kindness increases

the odds of early acceptance I've heard,
so I'll stress that for sure. And continue
my advanced studies in compassionate
joy (night class has evolved my point of view).

Financial assistance is not required,
but a quiet room's a must when I'm tired.

Shining A Light On It

Darkness understands that light is needed,
but light holds fast to its fear of the dark.
Night savors the heat that day leaves behind,
while day can hardly wait to kindle sparks

into a flame that leaves scars where it burns.
Darkness has a heart and sensitive skin.
Day has muscles and hedge funds to invest.
Night does not keep score. Day must always win.

The darkness was here in the beginning,
but light was born into this forced balance
of being and still fights to hold its place.
Thankfully, we can help light understand

a candle is enough to help us see.
We do not need to burn down all the trees.

Life Craft

Night then day. Night then day. Darkness. Then light
enough to watch the way my life flows by.
Endlessly by. Drifting in an ocean
of being, clinging to my life craft while

I drift. Mending my sails. Honing my planks.
Bailing out waves that I misjudged it seems.
Then mending my sail again. And honing.
Always honing. My thoughts. My plans. My dreams.

I'm asking for a friend— were we perfect
in the first place? Should I have accepted
life with open arms? Just plunged in and learned
to swim and dive and float as I drifted?

Would it have been enough to just be me—
and let life be the thing it wished to be?

This Is My Life

These walls. This window with its garden scene.
This moment as I sit and write these words.
This lingering sensation of a kiss.
These cold hands. This chittering of small birds

that I can hear but cannot see. These thoughts
that have never ever stopped appearing.
This ticking clock. These things matter to me
because they are what's here. Because they're me.

This is my life. This is the result of
my mother and father's brush with love that
never materialized. These are my
own brush strokes. I'm painting my own portrait.

The small birds have become memories now.
I've put away my pen. It lays fallow.

Measuring Growth

When I was small, and all the walls were tall
enough to stand against and measure each
season's growth with marks that made me feel big,
I was making progress which I could see.

In time, those marks plateaued. (In truth I must
admit they've lately fallen some.) Since then,
I've had to find some new way to measure
what it means to grow — be a bigger man.

That challenge has not been an easy one.
I looked everywhere I could to find an
idol I might pretend to be, though each
effort failed. I remained the same small man.

In time, my growth, I came to understand,
would expand each time I offered my hand.

Our Own Choosing

There is a reason why some of us are
forced to furtively squat behind broken
concrete while others rest on porcelain.
And there's a reason why some songs are sung

with a rasping pain that utterly stains
every bit of air in which it lingers.
There's a reason why some children suffer
while others have mothers who bring their

love with them as they light the path of life.
These reasons are clear to all of us. We
know them. Let's not pretend that we do not.
Instead, let's alter how we choose to see.

Because if we choose to see what made this,
we'll feel the weight. And the need to lift it.

Love, In All Its Forms

Much like the early morning hummingbird,
radiating spring's bright color array
as it sips cool nectar from a backyard
bleeding heart and begins another day,

I savor the flavor of beans roasted
six blocks away, and start my search for words
that clearly say what I've come to believe.
Which is that love, in all its forms, matters.

When we allow them to, our hearts connect
in ways we simply cannot understand.
Bridging the distances between all things.
Holding us up when there's no land to stand

upon — no boat in which to sail away.
Love matters. Not just today, but always.

That Singular Moment

... for Lisa

In that singular moment when my death
arrives for real, one thought alone will stir
within me. I'll look once more into your
eyes and then I'll rise to haunt all the air

that I no longer breathe — no longer need.
I will glimpse the two roads we have traveled,
yours and mine, on opposite sides of the
same stream. Always within view of the world

that connected us. Always within reach
of one another's heart. I'll watch the love
our lives shared begin to drift, infusing
life with its promises. Then I'll go,

leaving any remaining breath for you.
And as you breathe it in, we will endure.

Section II - Wistful Waka

house hunting

a couple young crows,
shopping for a neighborhood,
ponder my offer.
move from arbor to bird bath,
brush beaks; choose to keep looking.

sheets of nori

vinegar and rice
rolled tight with garden shiso
in sheets of nori.
simple offerings sustain
a happy gardener's heart.

bold strokes

blue scrub jay bursts through,
sweeps aside competition.
drinks and bathes and grooms—
lingers, collecting herself,
then flies. the garden quiets.

treasure map

unlike some gardens,
mine loves for squirrels to visit.
they conduct field tests
then rest, buddha-like, above
their search for buried treasures.

a welcome overstayed

the snow was lovely
as it fell. i enjoyed the
shoveling of it.
though now it feels somehow cold…
our friendship is uncertain.

losing hope

winter's chill hangs on
like sleep that won't release us,
as we long for warmth
with hearts aching to believe
that love remains possible.

twilight dialogue

i look to the past
as my brother slowly goes.
he's my last brother.
i'm grateful to have known him
much better these later years.

bittersweet melody

the death of small birds —
juncos, finches, chickadees
— all are heartbreaking.
their silence a reminder;
each moment's joy is fragile.

Section III - Acrostic Reflections

When I Lost My Way

What year it was when I finally
Had to admit I had lost my way
Evidently never became part of my scar...
Never left its indelible mark on my heart.

I do remember I was young. College years...

Learning to make my way in a world I could
Only pretend to care about because I could not
See any honesty in it. I could not feel any
Truth in what I had always been told.

My heart was open. I was looking for love.
Yet none appeared that I could believe in.

What saved me was cutting my boat loose.
Allowing myself to begin to freely drift through
Years of searching for the life I feel here now.

Remembering My Mother

Romanticized idealism was my mother's calling card. And
Every superficial perfection she imagined somehow became
My course syllabus— the things I was told to achieve.
Each time I won, regardless of the challenge, I was loved.
My failures received different, more shame-filled responses.
But my winning — bringing the light of recognition — gave her
Everything she believed she always deserved but was denied.
Right or wrong, the person my mother loved was the me
I always tried quite hard to be, but never fully achieved.
Not that things were always bad. They weren't. But the
Games we played were difficult to adapt to the wider world.

My way of interacting with life was influenced by her choices.
Yielding to those influences did not serve me well over time.

My mother's downfall, I believe, were the needs that carried
Over from her poor, uneasy childhood. From a learned response
To manipulate or deceive, and to live her dreams vicariously.
Her dreams became my childhood responsibility. She chose me.
Eventually, of course, the charade had to end. Now, my thoughts
Return to her for understanding more frequently than love.

Resting In Straw

Resisting the temptation to make a sound, or
Even to breathe, I'd curl up beneath a blanket of
Straw— near the top of a stack that was piled at least
Ten feet tall— while my older brother looked for me.
I was warm. I was alone. And I wished to remain so.
Nothing outside that cushion of aloneness could
Give me greater comfort. Of that I was certain.

I played games like that often as a child, even when
Nobody was looking for me. Looking back, I

Suppose I simply wanted to enjoy the time spent
Thinking about life. Pondering the nature of my
Relationship to the world around me. Only when I was
Alone could I do so. And since it was my favorite
Way to spend time, I often stole away to a place of repose.

My Sadie Years

More than anything else, I remember Sadie's eyes, and the
Yielding, comforting softness of her Springer coat. But it was her

Sad, searching eyes that ever looked to me for guidance,
And reassurance, and even for laughter in our later
Days, when we'd reached the point of no longer needing
Information beyond a glance or a gesture or a feeling flowing in
Either direction. Because she spoke to me as much as I to her.

Yesterday I spent a long while looking at the photos of Sadie
Ever present on my office wall. We had been connected, she
And me, in a way I still don't fully understand. And we still are,
Regardless of the fact that she's no longer here with me,
Save for her photos, and the box of ashes that now wait for mine.

Ballroom Dance Lessons

Before I was old enough to be too embarrassed
About it, my mother enrolled me in dance
Lessons — ballroom style — being taught at the
Ly-Kan Hotel in a town ten miles up the road.
Right away I figured out that I was the youngest
Of all the people present. And, at thirteen, definitely
Out of my element from a social standpoint, with
Mostly high school upperclassmen among the students.

Dancing, on the other hand, felt completely right
And natural to me. I listened to my mother's music
Nightly— folk tunes or orchestral versions of popular songs.
Coupled with that, I had somehow discovered jazz and
Enveloped myself in its emotional rhythms and moods,

Letting the music flow into my body. I couldn't stop that
Even if I had wanted to. And I so much didn't want to.
Sound became movement and movement set me free.
So few images now remain from those early, easy lessons.
Of course, after so long a time, that any remain at all should
Nourish my belief that the lessons I learned truly mattered, and
Should remind me that I can choose to let the music back in.

Walking Home From The Hospital

Who it was, specifically, to call the police and say
A student needed help, I still don't know. And most
Likely, I never will. It doesn't matter. I'm comforted to
Know someone cared enough to do so. They found me
In the worn, over-stuffed chair I lived in when I was
Not able to live anywhere else. Depression does that.
Gets you to find a spot where you feel least vulnerable.

How I got to the hospital psych ward was via cop car.
Over the course of the night, the counselor there convinced
Me, inadvertently, to develop a strategy that helped to
Eliminate any possibility I'd have to repeat the experience.

From the hospital back to home was a long fucking walk.
Right from the start I knew it would be and it was. But,
Overall, I didn't hate it. I kind of liked it. The cops leaving
Me to walk home pissed me off, but the walk itself was good.

The talk the counselor had with my folks led to an invite
Home. So I spent several months developing enough
Energy to chop wood and write poetry again. I got better.

How do I process all of this today? I don't really try anymore.
Over time, memories like these wear as thin as old news print...
So fragile they tear themselves to dust if you try to touch them.
Processing becomes more macro oriented when you age.
I blend thoughts together and develop nature-of-life hypotheses
That I can apply to my every-moment life. That's how I learn
About myself. One insight gained: there are things I've learned to
Like about feeling sad. Don't worry if at times I appear so.